WITH THE WIND

A Richard Jackson Book

WITH THE WIND

by Liz Damrell · pictures by Stephen Marchesi

ORCHARD BOOKS · NEW YORK

DB

Orchard Books, A division of Franklin Watts, Inc., 387 Park Avenue South, New York, NY 10016

Manufactured in the United States of America. Printed by General Offset Company, Inc. Bound by
Horowitz/Rae. Book design by Mina Greenstein. The text of this book is set in 18 pt. ITC Esprit Medium.
The illustrations are oil wash on canvas, reproduced in full color.

10 9 8 7 6 5 4 3 2 1

Library of Congress Cataloging-in-Publication Data
Damrell, Liz. With the wind / by Liz Damrell ; illustrated by Stephen Marchesi.   p.   cm. "A Richard
Jackson book"—Half t.p. Summary: A lyrical celebration of the power and majesty of horses and
horseback riding.
ISBN 0-531-05882-4   ISBN 0-531-08482-5 (lib. bdg.)
1. Horsemanship—Juvenile literature. [1. Horsemanship. 2. Horses.] I. Marchesi, Stephen, ill.
II. Title. SF309.2.D35 1991 799.2′3—dc20 89-48942 CIP AC

To my son, Devin,
and in memory of my parents,
Jack and Thelma Lee Teed

L.D.

For my wife, Christine

S.M.

He comes out to the field to see them run.

He puts his hand through the fence—
Carefully—

To touch their soft, strong faces.

915481

When it's time for him to ride
He closes his eyes
To feel the strength beneath him.

When he moves he's alive
To the sounds
The sights
The smells
The feel of the horse's life—

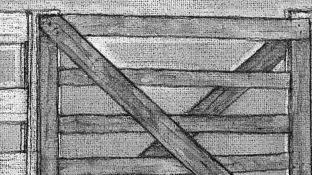
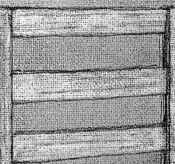

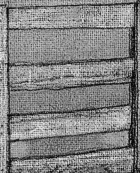
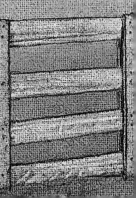

The Freedom.

Through the legs and the hooves
Of the horse

He can feel
The earth move
Away.

As the wind whips his hair
He sits in the air.

He rides through the field—

Among the horses

Among the riders

Alone with the joy—
Alone—

Feeling the power—
A Rider of Horses!

On the ground

People wait for him
To return.

He waves—
As if from a far distance—

Wanting them to know
What
A Rider of Horses
Feels—

Alone—
On top of the creature,
He knows.

Together,
With the riders—
He knows.

Going away—

What he has
Felt
Strengthening him

Beyond

Beyond the field

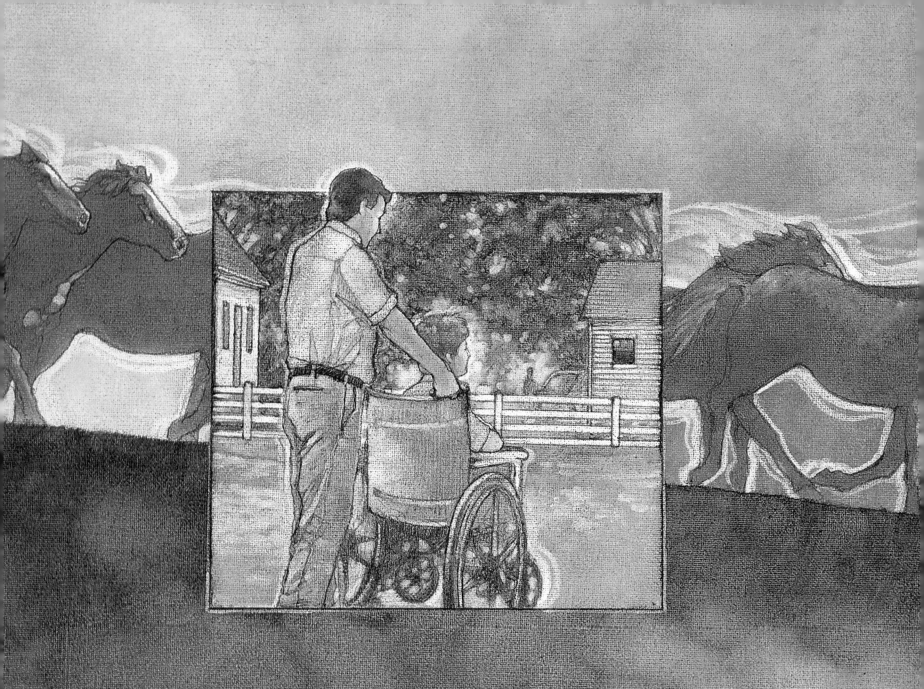

Where the Horses Run.